Play Foundations

Senses

Laura Henry and Jeanette Phillips-Green

Acknowledgements

© 2008 Folens Limited, on behalf of the authors.

United Kingdom: Folens Publishers, Waterslade House, Thame Road, Haddenham, Buckinghamshire HP17 8NT.
Email: folens@folens.com

Ireland: Folens Publishers, Greenhills Road, Tallaght, Dublin 24.
Email: info@folens.ie

Commissioning editor: Zoë Nichols
Managing editor: Jane Morgan
Design and layout: Infuze Ltd
Cover design: Infuze Ltd

Editor: Jane Bishop
Illustrations: Gaynor Berry
Cover illustration: Cathy Hughes

With thanks to the following for their permission to use extracts:
All Development matters statements and Aspects of learning quoted in this book are taken from *Practice Guidance for the Early Years Foundation Stage* (Department for Education and Skills) and are reproduced under the terms of the Click-Use Licence.
First published 2008 by Folens Limited.

Every effort has been made to contact copyright holders of material used in this publication. If any copyright holder has been overlooked, we should be pleased to make any necessary arrangements.

British Library Cataloguing in Publication Data. A catalogue record for this publication is available from the British Library.

ISBN 978-1-85008-339-9

Contents

Introduction   4
Planning chart   6
Assessment ideas   8
Observation hints   9

Chapter 1: I can touch
Cuddle songs   10
Squidgy ball   11
Pasta on a plate   12
Cornflour challenge   13
Material world   14
Feet first   15
Melting ice   16
Feel the rain   17

Chapter 2: I can see
Peek-a-boo!   18
Black and white   19
Fun to hide   20
Mirror, mirror on the wall   21
I see you   22
Sand in your hand   23
I spy   24
Shiny streamers   25

Chapter 3: I can smell
Smelly socks   26
Scented treasure   27
What's in the bag?   28
Sugar and spice   29
What's that smell?   30
Banana bonanza   31
Let's go on a walk   32
In our den   33

Chapter 4: I can hear
Hush, hush   34
Noisy box   35
Let's make a noise   36
Clap, clap your hands   37
Tipping towers   38
Squelch, squelch   39
Floating bubbles   40
Musical basket walk   41

Chapter 5: I can taste
Porridge taste   42
Vegetable discovery   43
Tongue fantastic   44
Hooray for purées   45
Fruitilicious   46
A taste of goodness   47
Five a day   48

Introduction

Who the book is for

This books forms part of the *Play Foundations* series which provides guidance for practitioners to set up quality play scenarios or activities with young children. It is written for all those who work with children under three in a whole range of settings – in the private, voluntary and independent sector and in children's centres. The activities will also adapt easily for childminders working with one or more children in their homes. It will be of special interest to all those settings and childminders who are working within the Early Years Foundation Stage (EYFS) and, of course, to parents*.

Learning through play

The activities in this book are based on the EYFS principles:

- Each child is unique and is a competent learner from birth.
- Positive relationships ensure that children learn to be strong and independent.
- Enabling environments play a key role in extending learning and development.
- Learning and development takes many different forms and all areas are connected.

You will find that the focus of the activities is on child-initiated learning and that the emphasis is on process rather than product. There are suggestions for using your guidance, your language and your support to promote the children's learning within the EYFS framework as they explore and play. Many of the activities can be enjoyed outside or inside. Being outdoors has a positive impact on children's sense of well-being and can help all aspects of development.

How to use this book

The book is divided into five chapters, each focusing on different ways in which children can enjoy and learn from 'senses'. The chapters are:

- I can touch
- I can see
- I can smell
- I can hear
- I can taste.

The activities

Each chapter has seven or eight activities including ideas for children of 0–11 months, 8–20 months, 16–26 months and 22–36 months. These age ranges will be familiar to those of you working with the EYFS framework. Some of the activities are designed for small groups of children and others are for use when you are working individually with the child. Always check for allergies and seek parental permission to take photos of the children.

You will see how all the activities are organised including the Areas of learning and development and aspects that they cover on pages 6 and 7. There are also suggestions for assessment and observation on pages 8 and 9 as well as within each activity.

Each activity is divided into the following sections:

- To help you plan *Enabling environments*, there is a section on *Setting up* outlining the resources you need and how to set up.
- *Getting started* describes how to organise the actual activity.
- *Let's talk!* provides ideas for talking with the children about their experiences including questions that can be asked and how to differentiate language to suit the children's varying abilities. There are also suggestions for making the most of assessment opportunities.
- Recognising *A unique child* and *Positive relationships* means making sure that self-esteem, confidence and relationships remain positive and there are *Top tips* for doing so.
- The *Differentiation* section includes ideas for personalising the learning by adjusting each activity to make it easier for children needing support or more challenging for others. This section will also be useful for planning inclusive activities for those children who have special or additional needs.
- *Further ideas* for each activity suggest ways of extending and enhancing learning and development opportunities.

How to support children as they learn

Supporting children's learning means setting up positive interactions and listening to what the children have to tell you, either with their voices, their reactions or their behaviour. Whatever stage a child has reached in their communication, they need space and time to respond to people, things and events around them and to know that practitioners are giving their full attention and encouragement. Spend a few seconds simply observing a child before moving in to interact, so that you can tune in to what they are doing, thinking about or reflecting upon at that moment.

Effective teaching means systematically helping children to learn so that they make connections in their learning – this involves knowing when to stand back as well as when to step in. Practitioners need to get to know each individual child well so they can judge the best kind of support and know when the child is ready to learn new skills. The use of the key person system allows children to form secure attachments and, from this sense of security, feel confident to explore and to develop further. The key person is the member of staff with whom the child has most contact and who shows special interest in the child through close interaction.

Working with parents

The EYFS emphasises that when parents and practitioners work together in early years settings, the results have a positive impact on children's development and learning. As you make progress through these activities, share your observations regularly with parents so that you can learn from each other. Newsletters, home-setting diaries and displays are all useful methods for doing this, making sure that everyone feels welcomed and included, that you respect diversity and that you communicate in ways that are accessible for everyone.

* Whenever the term 'parent' is used this is taken to include parents and/or the children's primary carers.

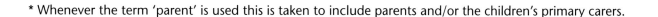

Planning chart

Use this chart to help with your planning. Each activity focuses on either one or two Area(s) of learning and development. These are highlighted by the stars shown on the chart. The Areas of learning and development are divided up into 'aspects' and the aspect(s) for each activity are also provided on the chart. On the activity pages you will also find a 'Development matters' objective for each activity.

The following key is used on the activity pages.

 PSED: Personal, social and emotional development

 CLL: Communication, language and literacy

 PSRN: Problem solving, reasoning and numeracy

 KUW: Knowledge and understanding of the world

 PD: Physical development

 CD: Creative development

Activities

I can touch

Activity	Page	Age	PSED	CLL	PSRN	KUW	PD	CD	Aspect of learning
Cuddle songs	10	0–11 months		★					Language for communication
Squidgy ball	11	0–11 months					★		Using equipment and materials
				★					Linking sounds and letters
Pasta on a plate	12	8–20 months						★	Being creative – responding to experiences, expressing and communicating ideas
Cornflour challenge	13	8–20 months				★			Exploration and investigation
Material world	14	16–26 months		★					Language for thinking
					★				Shape, space and measures
Feet first	15	16–26 months						★	Exploring media and materials
Melting ice	16	22–36 months				★			Exploration and investigation
				★					Language for communication
Feel the rain	17	22–36 months		★					Language for thinking
							★		Movement and space

I can see

Activity	Page	Age	PSED	CLL	PSRN	KUW	PD	CD	Aspect of learning
Peek-a-boo!	18	0–11 months					★		Movement and space
Black and white	19	0–11 months				★			Exploration and investigation
Fun to hide	20	8–20 months			★				Shape, space and measures
				★					Linking sounds and letters
Mirror, mirror on the wall	21	8–20 months	★						Dispositions and attitudes
				★					Language for communication
I see you	22	16–26 months			★				Numbers as labels and for counting
Sand in your hand	23	16–26 months						★	Exploring media and materials
I spy	24	22–36 months		★					Language for communication
						★			Time
Shiny streamers	25	22–36 months						★	Being creative – responding to experiences, expressing and communicating ideas
				★					Writing

Areas of learning and development

I can smell	Page	Age	PSED	CLL	PSRN	KUW	PD	CD	Aspect of learning
Smelly socks	26	0–11 months		★					Language for thinking
			★						Making relationships
Scented treasure	27	0–11 months			★				Numbers for labels and for counting
			★						Dispositions and attitudes
What's in the bag?	28	8–20 months				★			Exploration and investigation
							★		Movement and space
Sugar and spice	29	8–20 months						★	Being creative –responding to experiences, expressing and communicating ideas
				★					Writing
What's that smell?	30	16–26 months	★						Self-confidence and self-esteem
Banana bonanza	31	16–26 months						★	Exploring media and materials
Let's go on a walk	32	22–36 months		★					Writing
In our den	33	22–36 months						★	Developing imagination and imaginative play

I can hear	Page	Age	PSED	CLL	PSRN	KUW	PD	CD	Aspect of learning
Hush, hush	34	0–11 months						★	Creating music and dance
Noisy box	35	0–11 months				★			Movement and space
Let's make a noise	36	8–20 months			★				Shape, space and measures
Clap, clap your hands	37	8–20 months	★						Making relationships
				★					Reading
Tipping towers	38	16–26 months				★			Designing and making
							★		Movement and space
Squelch, squelch	39	16–26 months						★	Being creative – responding to experiences, expressing and communicating ideas
Floating bubbles	40	22–36 months		★					Reading
Musical basket walk	41	22–36 months						★	Creating music and dance
				★					Language for communication

I can taste	Page	Age	PSED	CLL	PSRN	KUW	PD	CD	Aspect of learning
Porridge taste	42	0–11 months				★			Place
				★					Language for communication
Vegetable discovery	43	0–11 months	★						Self-confidence and self-esteem
Tongue fantastic	44	8–20 months	★						Sense of community
Hooray for purées	45	8–20 months	★						Self-confidence and self-esteem
Fruitilicious	46	16–26 months						★	Exploring media and materials
				★					Writing
A taste of goodness	47	16–26 months	★						Self-confidence and self-esteem
Five a day	48	22–36 months			★				Shape, space and measures

Assessment ideas

Babies and young children are individuals first, each with a unique profile of abilities. All the planning that we do should flow from the observations that we make on an ongoing basis and these will help us to understand and consider their current interests, development and learning.

How to assess children

Observing children during their daily routines allows us to note their responses in different situations and to different people. In some settings, a specific Area of learning and development is targeted and the key person is asked to observe what stage the children in their care have reached over the next day or week, revisiting that Area from time to time. Others use sticky notes to record special moments in order to capture relevant observations. These can be collated later by a key person and entered into the ongoing records for the child. Others still make use of photos, daily diaries, activity feedback sheets or tracking records to capture the children's progress at different times. There is no prescribed method and practitioners find methods that suit their practice and the children and families concerned.

Planning for assessment

Through assessment you can see what stages the children have reached in their learning and development and therefore work out the best resources, opportunities and activities to plan next. Sometimes this might involve planning a specific activity to enable the child to take their learning that little bit further. Sometimes it will simply mean providing the right opportunities and observing the children as they play and learn independently. You will find a mixture of adult-led and child-led activities in the activity chapters with suggestions for you to observe and assess the children within the *Let's talk!* sections.

Using your assessments

Once you have observed the children at play, analyse your observations and highlight the children's achievements or their need for further support. Assessments are the decisions you make using what you have observed about each child's development and learning. Involve parents as part of the ongoing observation and assessment process and share your plans for the short-term (a week) and long-term (a term) planning. Your planning should always follow the same pattern – observe, analyse and reflect, then use what you have found out to plan next steps in the child's learning. In this way you can personalise the children's learning and make the most of their strengths, interests and needs.

The 'Look, listen and note' approach of the EYFS is a helpful tool when deciding what to observe and how. On the next page, this format has been applied to children learning about 'senses' so that you can begin to think about how your assessment and observations of children within this theme can feed back into your planning.

Observation hints

Here are some suggestions to start you off which will help you focus your observations and assessments when you are exploring and enjoying 'senses'.

Chapter heading	Look, listen and note
I can touch	Observe the way in which babies touch things with their fingers, hands and toes.
	Make a note of how the child needs support from you as their key person.
	Observe how the child's manipulative skills are developed and how they are able to grasp and hold objects.
	Make a note of the textures that the child prefers to touch.
I can see	Note how each baby moves their eyes to focus on an object.
	Note if the baby focuses on a particular pattern or object.
	Note how a baby touches and looks at you, your face, hair and so on.
	Observe how the child expresses likes and dislikes in what he or she sees.
	Make a note of how the child uses other senses to support the sense of sight – how they touch an object that they have seen for the first time.
I can smell	Notice how a baby gives attention to different smells and fragrances.
	Note how a child displays likes and dislikes to different smells.
	Make a note of a child's favourite smells and share the information with the child's parents.
I can hear	Notice how a baby turns his or her head when hearing a sound.
	Observe if the child has a preference for loud or soft sounds.
	Notice how a child is able to differentiate sound in the outdoor area.
I can taste	Write notes on how babies taste purées with their mouths and how they explore food with touch.
	Observe how children tell you about their likes and dislikes in what they eat.
	Note how a child uses body language and spoken language to show you their food preferences.

This activity helps children to develop communication skills and positive relationships with their key person.

Setting up

Set up a cosy area with rugs and cushions either indoors or outdoors. You could sit in a rocking chair with the baby, or rock the baby on your lap. Choose a CD/musical tape with nursery rhymes and lullabies, remembering to include songs from all different cultures and in the baby's own language.

Development matters
Communicate in a variety of ways including crying, gurgling, babbling and squealing.

Getting started

- Cuddle the baby in your arms, on your lap facing you or sit next to the baby, making eye contact and smiling. Gently say the baby's name and start humming a song or nursery rhyme. Then begin to sing the song, keeping eye contact, gently touching the baby, holding their fingers and so on. Say the baby's name and simple phrases such as *You can sing too.*
- Now play the CD or tape and sing or hum along with it. Keep cuddling, rocking and just being physically close to the baby. Remember to keep saying the baby's name and giving positive feedback to them with a gentle commentary such as *I really like your singing!* and give lots of smiles!
- Sing or say a nursery rhyme over and over again, always with the same emphasis, and move your body, for example, 'Twinkle, twinkle little star' moving your fingers up and down to make a star shape. The baby will begin to copy you!

Let's talk

For babies requiring more support, place their hand in yours and show them how to make the star shape, saying *This is how we make a star with our hands.* For babies needing a challenge, say *Can you show me how you make a star with your hands and fingers?* Note the different ways babies communicate, such as gurgling when happy or crying when unsettled and how they copy your actions, how they use their hands, fingers and so on.

Top tip

As the baby's key person, you will recognise the most suitable time of day to have this activity, for example, you may want to use it to settle the baby if they are tired. Provide tapes and tape recorders for parents so they can record familiar, comforting sounds, such as lullabies in the child's home language.

Differentiation

This activity will really stimulate the senses of the baby, whether the baby can just lie and listen, or sit or even begin to move around. Make this activity more challenging by playing games using the hands, such as 'Incy Wincy spider' and 'Jack and Jill', remember to keep giving lots of praise.

Further ideas

- Record the sounds that the baby makes and share these with the child's parents.
- Take photos of the baby enjoying this activity and display them in your cosy/sensory area.

Squidgy ball

This activity will develop the baby's fine motor skills of reaching and clutching.

Setting up
Set up a cosy area with rugs and cushions, indoors or outdoors, with plenty of space. Collect a variety of balls that are squidgy and soft to touch and place some in a treasure basket or box. Provide a mixture of brightly coloured balls and some black and white balls to give contrasts.

Development matters

Reach out for, touch and begin to hold objects.

Listen to, distinguish and respond to intonations and the sound of voices.

Getting started
- Cuddle the baby in your arms, on your lap, or sit next to the baby, making eye-contact and smiling. Choose a ball and gently move the ball through the baby's line of vision so that their eyes follow the movement.
- Next put the ball in the baby's hand or place the ball in front of the baby, encouraging them to reach for it. Now press the ball in your hand, saying *Let's feel the soft ball* or *Look, this ball is soft and squidgy.*
- Show the baby how to reach in to the treasure basket and take out the ball. When the baby copies you, give lots of positive feedback, say the baby's name, clap and smile. Encourage the baby to reach for the ball by moving the treasure basket further away from them.
- Have fun with the balls, roll them, throw them in the air, and throw them in to the basket and so on!

Let's talk
For those babies needing support, say *Let's touch the soft ball today with our hands.* For children requiring a challenge, ask *Which ball are you going to choose?* and *What can you do with the balls?* Notice what the baby does with the ball. Are they able to use their fingers to press the ball or do they need help from you? Note how young babies grasp and clutch at anything in their reach and the sounds they are making as they do this.

Top tip
Remember that whatever babies can do is their starting point. As their key person you can support the baby's learning, for example, as the baby plays with the ball, be supportive and be genuinely pleased with what he/she is doing.

Differentiation
This activity is appropriate for young babies whether they can lie, sit or stand. A very young baby will enjoy watching you move the ball from side to side and softly talking about what you are doing. Make this activity more challenging by encouraging the baby to reach for the ball and clutch something in both hands, or place the ball behind the baby to make them twist around.

Further ideas
- Place a large piece of paper on the floor, dip the ball in the paint and help the babies roll it over the paper.

Age range: 8–20 months

This activity will develop children's awareness that materials have different textures.

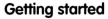
Setting up

Set up an area either indoors or outdoors and either put some cooked and cooled spaghetti and pasta (different shapes and colours) on plates on a plastic mat/low table or fill the water tray with it. Provide different textures by cooking some of the pasta well and keeping some more firm. Be aware of any children who may have an allergy to any of the ingredients in the spaghetti or pasta as they will naturally taste it too.

Development matters
Respond to what they see, hear, smell, touch and feel.

Getting started

- Talk to the children about the spaghetti and pasta, in particular the colours and how it moves when you touch it. Remember to make lots of eye contact and give plenty of smiles.
- Encourage the children to place their hands in the pasta and ask, *What does the pasta feel like? Is it hot or cold?* Support children who are anxious about putting the spaghetti and pasta on their hands by giving reassurance through cuddles and demonstrating what you can do with it: poke it, let it run through your hands, pick it up and drop it!
- If children want to taste the spaghetti and pasta let them, ask them what it tastes like and let them see you taste it too. Allow the children to take their time playing with the spaghetti and pasta as long as they are keen to do so.

Let's talk

Say, *Let's touch the spaghetti and pasta shall we?* For children requiring more support, say, *Where is the spaghetti or pasta? Is it in your hand?* For children needing a challenge, make up an action song to go with the activity, such as *Pasta on a plate, pasta on a plate, slippey, slidey, pasta on a plate.* Note how the children are responding to the texture of the spaghetti and pasta, their comments and body language. Are there any children who don't want to touch the spaghetti and pasta?

Top tip

This activity could be used as a calming activity, providing a relaxing sensory experience if you play quiet music in the background to enhance the atmosphere.

Differentiation

The youngest children may need you to help them pick up the spaghetti or pasta or you may need to hold the spaghetti or pasta in your hand and let them touch it. Challenge children to make spaghetti or pasta pictures by dropping the spaghetti or pasta on to paper and noticing the prints that they make.

Further ideas

- Provide spoons, saucepans and bowls for children to scoop and pour the spaghetti and pasta into. Children will also enjoy watching spaghetti run through colanders and spoons with holes in them.
- Enjoy pasta together at mealtimes and talk about the different shapes.

Cornflour challenge

This activity will help children to explore different consistencies through using cornflour.

Development matters

As they pull to stand and become more mobile, the scope of babies' investigations widens.

Setting up

Set up an area indoors or outdoors with plenty of space. Mix cornflour with water to make various consistencies, runny, thick, mushy and so on, and place it in trays on a low table. Provide objects that the children can dip into the cornflour such as pastry brushes, spoons and sponges. Be aware of any children who may have an allergy to cornflour.

Getting started

- Talk to the children about the cornflour, say *Let's play with the cornflour today.* As you do this, touch the cornflour with your fingers and hands. Now encourage the children to play with the cornflour: if children are able to stand by themselves you should sit next to them, if a child is unable to stand then they can sit on your lap.
- Let the children feel the different consistencies of cornflour in their fingers and hands and compare them together, saying *Look, this cornflour is runny/thick/squashy/mushy* and so on.
- Now pick up an object such as the brush and dip it, stroke it and press it into the cornflour. Say to the children, *What would you like to dip into the cornflour?* Give plenty of positive feedback to the children such as *I really like the way you are dipping your spoon into the cornflour* or *Well done, you are putting the brush into the runny cornflour.*
- If a child is anxious about having the cornflour in their hands, cuddle them and just let it run through your own hands.

Let's talk

Keep your commentary running, encouraging the children to describe what they are doing. For children requiring more support, say *Where is the cornflour? Is it on your fingers or is it on the brush?* For children requiring a challenge, ask *Can you tell me if the cornflour is runny or thick?* Note how the child plays with the cornflour, do they use their hands and fingers or do they choose to manipulate the cornflour with the objects?

Top tip

Talking and playing alongside children during activities like this, will help build positive relationships with them and help you to get to know each child better.

Differentiation

Remember that young children who are learning to stand and becoming more mobile need an adult close by to support them and for their safety. For children with mobility issues, the trays of cornflour can be placed in their lap or on the floor. To extend this activity let the children take the cornflour out of the packet themselves with a spoon and mix the cornflour with water.

Further ideas

- Try adding peppermint to the cornflour to add colour and smell to the activity.

Material world

**Age range:
16–26 months**

Provide opportunities for children to explore a variety of materials for colour and shape.

Setting up

Provide a large container such as a builder's tray, empty sand or water tray and fill it with a variety of fabrics in different textures and sizes (include voile, cotton, saris, African prints, silk, hessian and velvet). Place the container either indoors or outdoors where there is enough space for the children to explore the different materials.

Development matters

Are able to respond to simple requests and grasp meaning from context.

Enjoy filling and emptying containers.

Getting started

- Show the children the tray of materials and say *Look at all these materials! Shall we play with them today?* As you say this pull out some of the materials and hold them or let them fall through the air. Ask each child to take a piece of material from the tray, encouraging them to choose for themselves. As each child takes the material, give positive feedback through smiles and say *You have chosen the black and white material* or *I like the sari material you have chosen.*
- Allow plenty of time for this activity, so that the children are relaxed and have the opportunity to express themselves verbally and non-verbally. Also, allow the children to start conversations, give them thinking time and as the child's key person, help them to develop their interaction with you and other children.
- Talk about the colours, size, shape and texture of the material. For example, ask *How big is your piece of material? Do you like the colour of your material? What does your material feel like to touch?*

Let's talk

Keep your commentary going, noting the ways in which each child responds to the activity, remembering that young children's understanding is much greater than their ability to express their thoughts and ideas. For those children requiring more support, say *We are putting the material in your hand today. Doesn't it feel soft to touch?* For those children who need a challenge, ask them to find the red material, or the big, spotty piece of material and so on.

Top tip

As the child's key person it is important that you make opportunities to listen to the children.

Differentiation

For children requiring support, take a piece of fabric and either place it in the child's hand or gently run it up and down their arm, saying *Feel how soft this fabric feels.* For those children needing a challenge, let them take their fabric into the creative area and paint pictures or patterns on it. Remember too that young children use actions to express themselves as well as spoken language and that you should always respond positively to these actions.

Further ideas

- Place the materials in other areas of your setting, for example, in the role-play area so that the children can put the baby to bed by using material to cover the doll, teddy and so on.

Allow children to experience using their feet as a tool to be creative.

Development matters

Create and experiment with blocks, colour and marks.

LEARNING AND DEVELOPMENT

ENABLING ENVIRONMENTS

Setting up

Set up an area indoors or outdoors with trays or bowls filled with paint of various consistencies. Provide brushes of various sizes and large pieces of paper such as newspaper, wallpaper or sugar paper. You will need facilities to wash after the activity.

Getting started

- Take off your shoes and socks in front of the children, saying *We are going to play with our feet in the paint today!* Now dip one foot in the paint and then place it on the paper, making not only a print of your foot but also make all kinds of marks with your foot, for example, use just your toes, your heel, or make squiggles with your foot.
- Now help the children to take off their shoes and socks, saying *I wonder what pictures you will make with your feet today!* Remember, some children may not want to join in straight away, if at all, and you should respect the child's wishes. Encourage the child to 'have a go' at the activity through smiles, a positive commentary and showing that you are joining in the activity yourself.
- Encourage the children to dip their feet in the paint or paint their feet with the brushes and make marks on the paper. Allow sufficient time for the activity and value what each child can do. Keep a commentary running throughout this activity.

Let's talk

You should be mindful that children's responses to what they see, hear and experience through their senses are individual to them. For those children needing support, say *Look, we are painting our feet today. Can you show me how you paint your foot?* For those children requiring a challenge, say *Show me what you can do with the paint on your feet* or *I am watching how you use the paint today.* Make notes on how the child makes their creations and share this with parents.

A UNIQUE CHILD

POSITIVE RELATIONSHIPS

Top tip

Let the children see you enjoying this activity and 'having a go'. This will build positive relationships with you and the children and encourage them to express their individual creativity. A child with a visual impairment can still access this activity and feel the paint on their feet and so on.

Differentiation

Children at various stages of physical strengths and skills can enjoy the activity in their own way, just by sitting, watching and painting or walking and jumping in the paint. To extend the activity, you can play a CD/tape and encourage the children to dance to the music as they create their prints.

Further ideas

- Invite an artist into the setting, so that the children can observe and have first-hand experience of others making creations. Let the children be creative alongside the artist.

Melting ice

This activity will enable the children to observe and feel the changes that happen to ice as it melts.

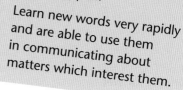

Development matters

Show an interest in why things happen.

Learn new words very rapidly and are able to use them in communicating about matters which interest them.

Setting up

Fill a sand or water tray with ice or place some ice on trays, include some in cubes, some that has been made in jelly moulds of different shapes and sizes and some that you have broken up. Buy bags of ice from a supermarket if necessary. Have towels ready to dry the children's hands. This activity will go on throughout the day, so that the children can observe the changes to the ice. Supervise the children to ensure they handle the ice for short periods only to avoid ice burns.

Getting started

- Say, *Look what's in the water tray today! What is it?* As you say this touch the ice and move your fingers and hands through it. Tell the children that ice is in the tray and encourage them to touch and play with it, remembering that some children may not want to join in straight away and will observe the other children. Keep your commentary running asking questions, such as *What does ice feel like? What happens if you hold the ice tightly in your hand? Have you seen ice before?* Allow time for the children to play with the ice, make comments and ask questions.
- Support the children in learning new vocabulary such as *wet, cold, slippery, hard* and so on.
- Allow the children to come and go to the tray as they wish, ensuring that there is always an adult supporting and interacting with them to notice the changes in the ice throughout the day.

Let's talk

For children needing support, say *This is ice in my hand. You have ice in your hand. Ice is cold and wet.* Keep your commentary running, encouraging the children to talk about ice and where and when they have seen ice before. For children requiring a challenge, ask *Can you tell me about the ice? What is happening to the ice?* Note how the children use words and actions to question what they see.

Top tip

Take photos of the activity and make an exciting display to share with parents. This will help to ensure that each child's family arriving at your setting feels welcomed and valued.

Differentiation

For those children who need support, place some ice in your hand and let them touch it, saying *You are touching the cold ice!* For children requiring a challenge place a variety of objects in the tray such as brushes, cloths, spoons and so on to extend their play. Ask the children *Can you tell me what is happening to the ice on the brush?* and so on.

Further ideas

- Display photos of ice, ice cubes, icebergs, ice-cream and so on in other areas of the setting (remembering they should be displayed at the children's eye level) to reinforce the activity.

Feel the rain

Help the children to enjoy the feel of the rain in the outdoor area on a rainy day.

Setting up

Make a collection of instruments from around the world. Wait for a rainy day! Ensure that you risk-assess the outdoor area for any hazards, before you take the children outside. Help the children change into their wellington boots and coats suitable for wet weather.

Development matters

Use language as a powerful means of widening contacts, sharing feelings, experiences and thoughts.

Gradually gain control of their whole bodies and are becoming aware of how to negotiate the space and objects around them.

Getting started

- On your chosen day, say *Let's go and play in the rain today!* Let the children run, jump, walk and so on in the rain. Join in with them, showing that you like to play in the rain as well.
- Record the sounds that the children make and the things that they are saying. Keep your own commentary running as well, asking the children questions about what they are doing and how the rain feels. Ensure that you make jottings and take photos of the children as they play in the rain, so that you can use them to plan further activities and track the children's development.
- Now encourage the children to choose and play an instrument from the basket while walking in the rain.

Let's talk

Have fun with the children, sing songs, shout out loud, whisper, call out their names and so on. For children requiring support, hold their hand and ask *What is the rain doing today?* and *Can you feel the rain on your hands?* Talk to the children about rainy days, whether they like wearing wellington boots and if they enjoy playing in the rain. Encourage children requiring challenge to describe the rain further. Ask questions such as *How does the rain feel on your face?* Ask them to think of rainy day words such as *splash*, *splish*, *splosh*, *dripping*, *raindrops* and so on. Note the vocabulary the children use, particularly if they begin to use new words that link with the activity.

Top tip

Remember that in order to be physically healthy, children don't simply need nutritious food. They also need access to the outdoors as well as loving, reassuring relationships with adults.

Differentiation

For children needing support, you should hold the child's hand and stay with them as they play in the rain. Follow their lead, playing alongside them to give them more confidence. To extend the activity, the children can use buckets, bowls, saucepans and so on to collect the rain. Ask, *How much water is collecting in your bucket?*

Further ideas

- Take some powder paints outside and let the children use the rain water to dip their brush in and mix the paints and then paint rainy-day pictures.

Introduce fun play for babies to encourage them to feel secure with you.

Setting up

Collect a variety of cardboard boxes of different shapes and sizes and arrange them on a rug or carpet, either indoors or outdoors, so that some are close together and some are far apart, mixing up the sizes.

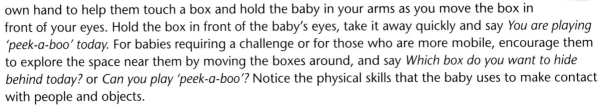

Development matters
Use movement and sensory exploration to link up with their immediate environment.

Getting started

- Cuddle the baby in your arms, on your lap facing you or sit next to the baby making eye contact and smiling. Say *Let's play peek-a-boo today, shall we?*
- Now start touching the cardboard boxes and talk about them, saying *I can see a big box* or *Look how small this box is.* Encourage the baby to touch the boxes, giving positive feedback to them with a gentle commentary, such as *You are looking at the very big box.*
- Next, hide behind the boxes, either by holding a small box up to your face or lying down behind a big box. Then either move the small box away quickly from your eyes or jump out from behind the big box and say *Peek-a-boo!*
- Repeat this movement changing the size of the boxes, remembering to change the sound of your voice. Be excited and laugh when you say *Peek-a-boo!*

Let's talk!

Encourage the baby to focus on your face as you say *Peek-a-boo!* Notice how the baby touches the boxes if they are able to reach out and touch them. For younger babies, use your own hand to help them touch a box and hold the baby in your arms as you move the box in front of your eyes. Hold the box in front of the baby's eyes, take it away quickly and say *You are playing 'peek-a-boo' today.* For babies requiring a challenge or for those who are more mobile, encourage them to explore the space near them by moving the boxes around, and say *Which box do you want to hide behind today?* or *Can you play 'peek-a-boo'?* Notice the physical skills that the baby uses to make contact with people and objects.

Top tip

Remember, children learn better by doing things themselves, ideally with other people who are more competent, rather than simply being told what to do.

Differentiation

All babies will benefit from this activity as their emotional needs are being met by having a warm supportive relationship with you. Children who are more physically able will explore the boxes by themselves and gain more confidence in what they can do.

Further ideas

- Attach photos of the babies to the boxes and point to them as you play 'peek-a-boo'.

Black and white

Use strong patterns and contrasting colours as an exciting stimulus for babies who are starting to explore.

Development matters
Use movement and senses to focus on, reach for and handle objects.

Setting up

Collect black and white resources: include black and white throws, fabrics, cushions, boxes and toys. Arrange the resources in a cosy, attractive way in an appropriate corner/area of the room. You could also include a black and white treasure basket by filling a basket approximately 40cm wide and 12cm deep with a mixture of safe, black and white items.

Getting started

• Sit in the black and white area with the baby either on your lap facing you or sitting next to you, making eye contact and smiling. Choose an object from your collection and move it slowly through the baby's line of vision, so that their eyes can follow the movement. Talk to the baby about the object.
• Now either cuddle the baby, allowing them time to just look around at all the black and white objects or sit quietly next to the baby while they reach out and choose objects for themselves. If you have a treasure basket allow the baby to choose an item from the selection.
• If the baby shows a particular interest in an object, talk about the object, for example, say *You are looking at the black and white material* or say the baby's name and *We are looking at the black and white zebra together.*

Let's talk!

Babies will enjoy exploring the objects using their sight to notice the contrasting black and white items. Your role as the key person is to support younger babies by keeping a gentle commentary running, naming a few of the objects and saying *Look at the black and white dog!* For babies who need a challenge, offer encouraging words and ask *What are you looking at? Which of the black and white things do you like playing with?* Notice how young babies use their senses to investigate objects as well as how they touch your face or your hair.

Top tip

Show the parents your black and white area, explaining why you have set it up for their baby, how they use the area and what the baby is learning from it. The babies will feel an increased sense of belonging in a setting when their parents are also involved there.

Differentiation

All young babies will benefit from the stimulus of the black and white area as they can explore it and the resources in their own way. Support babies who have a visual impairment, by gently brushing the black and white objects on the back of the baby's hand, feet or face. Challenge babies to explore the area independently when they are able to.

Further ideas

• Remember to include black and white photos of the babies' families and familiar objects in your room.

Fun to hide!

**Age range:
8–20 months**

Children can learn about different sizes by exploring a range of familiar objects in your setting.

Setting up

Collect a variety of objects that are obviously big or small, such as a big box, a big train, a small car and also picture books showing big and small objects such as a big cat and a small kitten. Hide the objects in your outdoor area (check for hazards) if possible or indoors if necessary.

Development matters

Recognise big things and small things in meaningful contexts.

Enjoy babbling and increasingly experiment with using sounds and words to represent objects around them.

Getting started

- Take the children into the outdoor area and talk to them about big and small things. Point out some big and small objects in the outdoor area, for example the big tree or the small flower.
- Play a game with the children, saying *Who can make themselves big?* and as you say this stretch up high and open your arms wide, then say *Let's make ourselves small and curl up into a ball.* Encourage the children to copy you and give positive re-enforcement when they do with smiles, saying the name of the child and *Well done, you do look big now* or *Wow, look how small you are today!*
- Next tell the children that some big and small things are hiding and challenge them to help you find them. Keep a commentary running throughout the activity and praise the children when they find an object. Comment on the relative size of each item, *What a big car you have found* or *That's a tiny little teddy isn't it?*

Let's talk!

For children needing support, hold the object in one hand and say *I am holding a big ball today, can you say 'big ball'?* Ask children requiring a challenge open questions, such as *Can you tell me about the ball you have found?* Notice how a child holds their arms out wide to gather up a big teddy and brings their hands together to pick up a small ball.

Top tip

Encourage the children to help each other to find objects, as making friends and getting on with others helps children to feel positive about themselves and promotes emotional well-being.

Differentiation

Support younger children by carrying them if necessary or holding their hands so they can join in. Children with English as an additional language will find the different-sized objects a useful prop to support their communication. Challenge children to find an item bigger or smaller than one you show them.

Further ideas

- Encourage parents to play with or hide big and small objects at home to extend the child's learning and enhance home-setting links.
- Set up a table-top display of items of different sizes such as a big car and a small car, a big book and a small book.

Mirror, mirror on the wall

Have fun looking at yourselves and each other in mirrors!

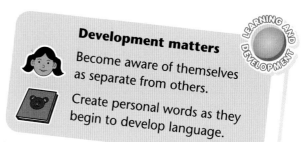

Development matters

Become aware of themselves as separate from others.

Create personal words as they begin to develop language.

Setting up

Collect a variety of safety mirrors and place them on a rug or a low table or hang them on a wall at a low level. Create a cosy area with rugs, throws and cushions, either indoors or outdoors where there is no 'through traffic'.

Getting started

- Encourage the children to sit on a cushion or sit them on your lap facing you. Play a game with the child's name, saying *I can see Katie today* or *Where is Billy today?* Keep your commentary running and extend the game saying *Where is my nose? Where is Ravi's nose?* pointing to your nose and the child's nose. Repeat with other parts of your and the child's face: eyes, nose, mouth and so on.
- Now say *Let's look in the mirror and see what we can see!* Either hold the mirror up to the child's face, or encourage and help more mobile children to look in the mirror themselves.
- Talk to the children about what they can see. Playfully help them recognise that they are separate and different from others, pointing to their eyes, nose and fingers in turn. Remember to be quiet at times so you can hear the child's sounds and words as they look at their reflection.

Let's talk!

Support children by following their lead as they look in the mirror: if the child points to their fingers for example, say *You are looking at your fingers in the mirror!* or *Look, I can see Emma's curly hair.* For children requiring a challenge, say *Tell me what you can see in the mirror* or *I am wondering what you are looking at today.* Note the sounds or words the children make as they look at their reflections.

Top tip

Each baby and child will develop in individual ways and at varying rates, allow each one to do the things they can, help them with the things they cannot quite manage and do things for them they cannot do for themselves.

Differentiation

For children needing your support, look in the mirror and talk about yourself, saying *Look at my curly hair* and so on. To extend the activity, put some yoghurt on the mirrors and let the children make marks on them with their fingers, revealing their own faces as they wipe the yoghurt away (check for any allergies).

Further ideas

- Place a treasure basket of shiny things such as spoons and saucepans so that the children can see in the mirror what they are holding and looking at and look at their reflections in the back of the spoon!

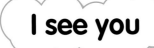

I see you

Children can develop counting skills by sort items in a variety of ways.

Setting up

Gather a selection of clothing items such as gloves, socks, shoes and hats and put them in a large basket or box on a rug either indoors or outdoors. Ensure that the area is cosy with cushions and throws arranged in an attractive way.

Development matters

Say some counting words randomly.

Getting started

- Encourage the children to come and join you in the area by saying *Look at what I can see in the basket.* Ensure that the children are not sitting too close together and that the basket or box of resources is within easy reach of them so they can choose things from it.
- Say *Look how many things are in the basket! What can you see?* to encourage the children to join you. Encourage the children to pick items out and name them, or choose an item and hold it up for the children to name and describe.
- Now say, *Can you help sort all these things out?* and take out one of a pair of gloves or shoes and say *I'm trying to find the gloves. What are you going to do?* encouraging them to suggest finding the pair for you.
- Sit back and allow the children to play with the items, exploring, sorting and counting the clothing. Continue a running commentary as they play.

Let's talk!

Encourage the children to look at you as they talk to you about what they are playing with and sorting. For children needing support, choose an item with them and say *Look we have found a hat* or *We are looking for a shoe together.* For children requiring a challenge, ask them to find two shoes or one shoe and one hat, and so on. Note children's awareness of number during the activity, such as the number words used and when and why they use them.

Top tip

Remember that language, thinking and learning are interlinked and you as the child's key person are supporting this by allowing the appropriate time and space for young children to develop mathematical language and ideas. If a child has a physical impairment and is in a wheelchair, for example, they can have a basket of objects on their lap to sort.

Differentiation

For those children requiring support, sort out the objects with them saying *Can you find a shoe like I have?* or *Where is the hat?* To extend the activity, hide the objects around the room or outside and say *Who can find me the red hat?* and so on.

Further ideas

- Take the basket/box of clothing into the role-play area for children to dress up in too.
- Provide a basket/box of different textured fabrics from around the world for children to sort.

Sand in your hand

Children will enjoy exploring a range of textures using their senses.

Setting up

Collect a variety of resources of different textures such as sand, play dough, jelly and shaving foam and include unusual or interesting materials such as raffia, string, or water-based glues with colour added. Place a small amount of each resource on a tray or plate and put these on the floor or on a low table, either indoors or outdoors. You will need wipes and towels to dry the children's hands. Check for allergies to any of the materials.

Development matters

Create and experiment with blocks, colour and marks.

Getting started

- Gather the children and say *What can you see today? Look at all these things to play with!* Say *I can see some sand and I can see some jelly* and point to the resources in turn. Talk about the textures and colours that they can see.
- Next encourage the children to play with and explore each resource. Allow them to each spend as much time as they want exploring, playing, and touching each resource.
- Listen to what the children say and accept their comments about each resource. If a child doesn't want to play with any of the resources, accept this wholeheartedly and reassure the child with positive language and smiles.

Let's talk

Recognise that every child's learning journey is unique to them and show them that you are interested in what they are doing, ask questions, make gentle comments and listen carefully to what they are saying. If a child is reluctant to join in or needs support, place something such as the shaving foam in your own hands and talk about what it looks like and how it feels. Pick up the child's hands and encourage them to touch the shaving foam with you. For the child needing a challenge, say *Tell me how the sand feels in your hands* or *What does the jelly feel like?* Notice the inventive ways in which children play with the different textures and what they enjoy/dislike.

Top tip

Give each child the time to think about what they want to do, and to express their wishes, rather than stepping in to help and making decisions for them.

Differentiation

For children needing support, sit close to them and play with the resources together, taking your lead from them about which resources interest them. To extend the activity, empty a water tray and put all of the resources in it for the children to look at and play with. Include spoons, bowls and brushes for them to fully explore the resources.

Further ideas

- Take photos of each child exploring the various textures to put into their learning journals/profiles, with accompanying observations and share these with parents.

I spy

The children can learn some new words while they have fun with this game.

Setting up
Find pictures and photos that show objects and events that will be familiar to children such as a house, a chair, eating a meal, a car, going swimming and so on. Ensure they represent all the cultures of the children in your group, for example, include a wok, or pictures of different types of bread such as naan or pitta bread. Place the pictures and photos on the floor or a rug.

Development matters
Learn new words very rapidly and are able to use them in communicating about matters which interest them.

Anticipate specific time-based events such as mealtimes or home time.

Getting started
- Gather the children and say *Look at all these pictures and photos on the rug, can you see them?* Let the children play with the pictures, encouraging each child to look carefully at them and choose their own. Ask the children to tell you what their picture or photo is, allowing them time to name the object and talk about the event.
- Say *We are going to play I spy today!*, hold up a picture or photo and say *I spy with my little eye a chair* or *I spy with my little eye somebody swimming in the sea.* Then hold up one photo at a time and ask the children to tell you and talk about what the object is, or what is happening in the photo.
- Now name a child and ask them to hold up a photo for everyone to say what the object is or what the picture is about.

Let's talk
For children needing support, hold the photo with them and say *Victor spies, with his little eye a picture of a …* For children requiring challenge, ask open questions such as *Can you tell me what you can spy with your little eye?* Note how children begin to ask questions and use new vocabulary.

Top tip
Make this activity fun, laugh with the children as you play to demonstrate how to play with and get on with others, whether it is other children or adults.

Differentiation
To support children just choose one or two items such as the 'car' and the 'house' and use these to play the game, ensuring that you sit closely to the child, so that they feel supported. To extend the activity, let the children choose objects and hide them for other children to find either indoors or outdoors.

Further ideas
- Put real objects of those displayed in the pictures and photos in the role-play area, for example, a wok, clocks, or a hairdryer, for the children to play with, and reinforce their learning.
- Share some simple picture books that provide pictures and single words to introduce new words.

Shiny streamers

Children will develop their creativity moving to music and playing with shiny material in this activity.

Setting up

Gather some shiny material such as silver foil, ribbon and so on and make streamers by cutting out strips of the materials and attaching them to a cardboard tube. Alternatively you can glue the shiny materials on to a thick piece of card to mould into a small wristband for the children. Choose an appropriate CD/musical tape. Make sure you have your camera!

Development matters

Seek to make sense of what they see, hear, smell, touch feel.

Distinguish between the different marks they make.

Getting started

- Take the children into the outdoor area and start playing the CD or tape. Encourage them to dance to the music and join in with them by holding on to their hands or dancing alongside them. Let the children see you are enjoying the activity as this will encourage them to take part.
- Give each child a streamer and show them how to wave, swirl and play with them. Keep your commentary running, talking to the children about what they can see. Talk about the colours and how the light makes them shine.
- Allow the children to explore what the streamers can do and be positive towards them through smiles, words and copying what they are doing with the streamers. Take photos of the children playing with the streamers.

Let's talk

Show an interest and value what the children do, saying *Well done, I really like how you are playing with the streamer* or *Wow, look at the lovely patterns you are making with the streamer.* For children requiring support, hold on to their hand and wave the streamer with them, saying *Look how you are waving the streamer.* For those children needing a challenge, ask them to describe what they are doing with the streamer, *Tell me how you like to play with your streamer.* Note how children use gestures in response to their experiences, for example, a child may jump up and down when they are excited.

Top tip

This activity supports the child's health and well-being as it gives them access to the outdoor environment with the support of a loving relationship with their key person.

Differentiation

For those children needing support, hold on to the streamer with the child and wave it in the air together. To extend the activity, take a box of fabrics, paper of different textures and so on and let the children make their own streamers.

Further ideas

- Take large sheets of paper outside and ask the children to mark-make pictures of the movements they have made with the streamers.
- Print and mount the photos of the children and make a display for parents to view.

Introduce new smells to babies with this fun activity.

Setting up

Gather together some socks of different sizes, colours and with different patterns on them. Fill the socks with fragranced items such as talcum powder, curry powder, thyme, sage, parsley, coffee, soap and lemon. Be aware of any allergies to materials. Tie the top of each sock with some thin ribbon so that the fragrances can't fall out. Set up a cosy, attractive area either indoors or outdoors with a rug and cushions and arrange the socks on the rug or place them in a basket.

Development matters

Are intrigued by novelty and events and actions around them.

Learn by interacting with others.

Getting started

- Either cuddle a very young baby in your arms, sit the baby on your lap facing you or sit next to the baby, ensuring that they are supported by cushions. Sing a nursery rhyme to the baby, encouraging older babies to join in with you.
- Now pick up one of the socks, hold it to your nose and say *Mmm, this smells good!* Hold the sock to the baby's nose very gently and say *What can you smell?* Then hold a different sock to the baby's nose, being very gentle and taking your time. Encourage more mobile babies to pick up the socks by themselves, praising them when they do, as they reach for and grasp them.
- You can also place a sock in the baby's hand and watch how they explore it. Keep your commentary running, talking to the baby about the different smells in the socks ensuring that you vary the intonation of your voice.

Let's talk!

For babies requiring support, say *I can smell a lemon* as you hold the sock to the baby's nose. Repeat this with the other fragrances, always naming what you can smell. For those children requiring a challenge, say *I wonder what that smell is, can you tell me?* or *What is in this smelly sock?* Watch and listen to how the baby shows you the smells they like and dislike. Listen to the range of sounds the baby makes, such as squealing or babbling.

Top tip

Babies are especially interested in other people and in communicating with them, using eye contact, crying, cooing and gurgling to have conversations. As the baby's key person, you can have 'conversations' even with very young babies.

Differentiation

For children who need support with this activity, just focus on one or two fragrances. To extend the activity, let babies smell the socks to find two that have the same smell.

Further ideas

- Hang a line of ribbon up at a low level with a basket of pegs underneath it. Peg the 'smelly socks' on the line yourself, talking to the babies as you do so or help more mobile babies to peg the socks on the line themselves.

Scented treasure

Let babies go exploring with this activity to sniff out some treasure.

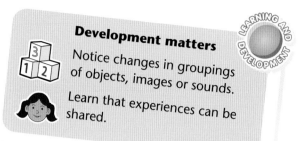

Development matters

Notice changes in groupings of objects, images or sounds.

Learn that experiences can be shared.

Setting up

Set up four treasure baskets: in one basket place a lemon, in another two fir cones, in the third three of the 'smelly socks' from page 26 and in the fourth basket an orange. You can vary the items on another occasion. Check for allergies. Set up a cosy area with cushions and throws and place the baskets on a rug.

Getting started

- Either cuddle a very young baby in your arms, sit the baby on your lap facing you or sit next to the baby, ensuring that they are supported by cushions. Sing a nursery rhyme or lullaby to the baby, ensuring that you always maintain eye contact.
- Now say *I wonder what these things are in the baskets?* Encourage more mobile babies to look in to the baskets with you. Pick up the lemon from the basket and hold it up to the baby's nose saying *Mmm, I can smell a lemon.* Allow the baby time to smell the lemon, showing approval with smiles.
- Now let the babies play with the objects in the other baskets. Sit back and watch how they investigate and explore what is in each basket. Help a baby on your lap by taking an object out of a basket and holding it to the baby's nose to smell.
- Begin to comment on what the baby is doing, say *You are looking at the smelly socks. What can you smell?* or *What does the orange smell like? Do you like the smell?*

Let's talk!

For babies needing support, place an object in their hands, gently brush it across their hand and then hold it to their nose, saying *This is the lemon* or *Mmm, smell the sock.* For children requiring a challenge, ask them about what they are smelling *What have you got in your hands? How does it smell?* Notice how the baby gives attention to the smelly objects and whether they notice the change in the quantities of objects they see.

Top tip

This activity helps you to bond with the baby as their key person, as you join in the sensory activity together.

Differentiation

A gentle stroke on the back of the hand will encourage reluctant hands to open! For babies who find using two hands difficult, ensure that they are really supported either by you or the cushions, so that they can focus on reaching for an object without falling over. Challenge children to find the items from the basket as you name them.

Further ideas

- Take the baskets into the creative area and let the children dip the objects in paint and print with them on paper or materials with your support.

What's in the bag?

Have fun putting smelly things in and out of bags!

Setting up

Make a collection of bags of different shapes, sizes and materials (not plastic) ensuring that they are safe and have no rough edges or loose buttons. Fill the bags with resources that have different fragrances such as: lemons, cheese, coffee, pot-pourri, a cabbage and include items from other countries such as yam or mango. Check for allergies to any of the resources. Set the bags out in an area either indoors or outdoors, where there is space for the children to move and explore them.

Development matters

As they pull to stand and become more mobile, the scope of babies' investigations widens.

Use their increasing mobility to connect with toys, objects and people.

Getting started

- Gather the children together and show them the bags, open one up and say *Look, there's some cheese in this bag. Who wants to smell the cheese?* Pass the bag around for each child to smell the cheese; some will want to taste it as well!
- Now let the children play with and investigate what they can find and smell in the other bags, giving them plenty of time and space in which to do this. Keep a commentary running throughout the activity, especially to comment on what the child is smelling, for example, *You are smelling the cabbage!* or *You have taken the smelly cheese out of the bag.*
- Support the children with taking things in and out of the bags and moving themselves to investigate the collection.

Let's talk!

Give support by saying, *Let's look in the bag together, what's that smell?* and taking out the objects together. For children needing a challenge, expand their vocabulary by naming the objects in the bags together, remembering to ask open questions such as *Tell me about your smelly bag. What is in it?* Note what holds the child's interests and the ways in which they investigate and manipulate objects through their senses.

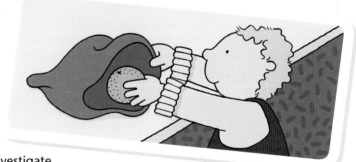

Top tip

When children feel happy and secure they are confident to explore and to try out new things. You as the child's key person have the special responsibility for giving them the reassurance to feel safe and cared for so that they will explore the bags and learn through play.

Differentiation

To support children, sit close to them and show them just one or two objects, taking your time and noting how they respond. To extend this activity, encourage the children to put things in and out of the bags and invite them to find things to go in the bags.

Further ideas

- Take a small group of children to the shops to buy items such as bread to make sandwiches or fruit for their snack, letting the children put items in bags to bring back to the setting.

Sugar and spice

Introduce some sweet and spicy smells to the children to help them learn the difference between them.

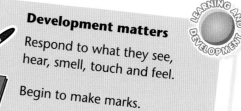

Development matters

Respond to what they see, hear, smell, touch and feel.

Begin to make marks.

Setting up

On a low table place a variety of resources, some that smell sweet and some that are spicy. These could include: sugar, coffee, jam, honey, curry powder, chocolate spread and pepper and sweet/spicy smelling things from other cultures. Check for allergies to any of the items. Place the resources directly on the table, so that the children can have a sensory experience through accessing all the different fragrances at the same time.

Getting started

- Maintain strict supervision at all times with this activity to prevent the children tasting inappropriate items (curry powder or non-edible items).

- Invite the children to join you at the table, saying *Look at all these sweet and spicy things on the table. Let's play with them!* Now start touching the resources on the table with your hands and fingers. As you do this, talk to the children about what you can smell, say *I'm running my fingers through the sugar* and so on. Encourage the children to play with the resources and smell them.

- Join in with the children, making marks in the jam or honey to encourage early writing skills. Say the names of the resources, and ask them what smells sweet and what smells spicy.

- Make sure that the children wash their hands thoroughly after the activity and praise them for not tasting when you asked them not to.

Let's talk!

For children needing support, play with one of the resources in your hand and then gently place some in their hands, saying *We are playing with the jam together. It smells sweet.* For the child requiring a challenge, say *Can you find me something that smells sweet/spicy? Do you know what this is called?* Note the child's favourite smell and remember to share this with the child's parent.

Top tip

Play some quiet music in the background, as this will make the activity a therapeutic one and give the children a rest from stimulation for a while.

Differentiation

To simplify this activity, let the children watch you as you smell the different fragrances. Just hold one sweet and one spicy fragrance to their noses to sniff. Make this activity more challenging by asking the children to find a new fragrance for you in the setting, saying *Can you find me something that smells sweet?*

Further ideas

- At snack time invite the children to help you make a sweet snack one day and a spicy one another, reinforcing the words *sweet* and *spicy*.

What's that smell?

Take to the great outdoors to find some new smells together.

Setting up

Place a selection of fragranced resources such as tea bags, jelly, ice-cream, shaving foam, flowers and herbs in trays or boxes. Place these in different places around your outdoor area, remembering to risk-assess the area first for hazards. Check for any allergies to resources.

Development matters

Explore from the security of a close relationship with a caring and responsive adult.

Getting started

- Take the children outside and let them play in the outdoor area for a few minutes. Join in with their play, running, jumping and having conversations with them. Now call the children to you, saying *I'm going on a smelly walk, who wants to come with me?*
- Find one of the trays or boxes and say *There is something smelling in this tray, I wonder what it can be?* Get down on the ground and smell what is in the tray, encouraging the children to do the same. Now ask the children to search for the other trays or boxes and tell you what they have found and how things smell.
- Encourage each child through positive comments, smiles and by holding their hand.

Let's talk!

Keep talking to each child during this activity, appreciating their efforts when they show an understanding of new words and phrases. For the child requiring support, take their hand, lift up the tray for them to smell what is in it and say *We can smell the tea bags together* or *Well done, you are smelling the flowers.* For children needing a challenge, say *Can you find me the tray with the shaving foam in?* Notice how the children grow in confidence as they find the different resources and tell you how they smell.

Top tip

Remember that children are likely to be much less independent when they are in new situations, so you as their key person should reassure each child during this activity, giving lots of praise and be genuinely pleased when they find the tray or box.

Differentiation

Simplify the activity by focusing on one or two trays and smells only. To challenge children, ask them to find other fragrances in the outdoor area, such as plants, sand and so on.

Further ideas

- Plant some mustard and cress seeds in yoghurt pots with the children, watch them grow and let the children make mustard and cress sandwiches with you.
- Take the children outside to smell the trees and plants at different times of the year and according to the weather. When it has just rained, for example, smell how fresh the trees and plants are.

Banana bonanza

Have fun with this printing and sensory activity with bananas!

Development matters

Create and experiment with blocks, colour and marks.

Setting up

Pour different coloured paints into a large tray, collect some paper of different colours, shapes and sizes and set the materials up on a low table or a plastic sheet, indoors or outdoors. Buy lots of bananas and cut them up into various sizes. Check for allergies and use alternative fruit if necessary.

Getting started

- Encourage the children to come and join you in the activity by saying *Mmm, I can see lots of lovely bananas! Who would like to come and see them?*
- Now ask the children if they like bananas and pass round a piece of banana for each child to smell, touch and taste. Talk to them about how the banana smells and tastes, asking questions to prompt their responses.
- Next, take a piece of banana, dip it into the paint and then make prints on the paper with it. Now ask the children if they would like to print and make patterns with the banana, showing them how to hold the pieces carefully but without squeezing them too hard. Ensure no further tasting goes on once the banana has paint on it!
- Support each child with their pattern-making for as long as they are interested and do not force them to continue if they are reluctant. Keep talking about how banana smells as the children are painting.

Let's talk!

Provide support by sitting next to children, placing the banana in their hands and saying, *Let's paint with the banana. What pictures will we make?* For children requiring a challenge, ask them to tell you about the patterns they are making with the banana. Say, *Can you tell me about the pattern how you are making?* Note how the children create their pictures and share this with the child's parents.

Top tip

Remember that warm, trusting relationships with knowledgeable adults support children's learning more effectively than any amount of other resources.

Differentiation

Support children by helping them hold the banana and making a pattern. To make this activity more challenging, let the children try folding their paper into a card and then making patterns with their banana on the card.

Further ideas

- Provide a selection of different fruits and vegetables for the children to paint and print with.
- Use bananas for simple cooking activities together such as mashing them for sandwiches and adding them to fruit salad.

Let's go on a walk

Put your best feet forward for a sensory walk together.

Setting up
Decide on a suitable route for a sensory walk, whether you are in the country or the town, and make the necessary arrangements with permission and helpers. Collect papers of different sizes and colours and various mark-making materials such as chalks and crayons.

Getting started
- Tell the children that you are taking them on a walk to find out what they can smell, touch, hear and see. Encourage them to think about what they will smell in particular along the way, making suggestions such as flowers or farmyard smells in the country and traffic and machinery in a town.
- Set off on your walk and point out landmarks or items along the way that they can see, smell and hear such as a car parked by the roadside, some flowers growing in a garden and so on. Allow the children to stop and touch things provided it is safe to do so.
- Find a suitable place to stop, where the children can sit down. Hand out the materials and encourage the children to use mark-making to make a picture to record their walk, choosing something they have seen, heard, smelled or touched.

Development matters
Distinguish between the different marks they make.

Let's talk!
During the walk ask questions and listen to the children's responses. When they are mark-making, ask them what their pictures represent, saying *Tell me about your picture and the marks you are making.* Help children needing support to select a suitable piece of equipment, *Would you like to use a crayon or chalk?* For children requiring a challenge, say *I am wondering what you are drawing* or *What did you see on the walk? Can you draw a picture of it?* Note what children tell you about the marks they make.

Top tip
Remember that by observing and listening to each child, you can discover what they like to do and recognise when they feel confident, scared or frustrated.

Differentiation
Support children by going for a very short walk with the purpose of finding one particular smell, such as some flowers. To challenge children, provide clipboards and invite them to stop during the walk to record what they wish to.

Further ideas
- Take photos of the walk, and display them attractively with the children's comments alongside them for the parents to see. Display the children's mark-making as well alongside the photos.
- Try and arrange a visit to a different locale: if you live in the country take a bus ride to a busy town, or if you are in the town arrange a visit to a country park or a farm.

In our den

Have fun making a den outdoors and use it for creative play.

Setting up

Set up a den in the outdoor area, either using a tent or a big cardboard box with a blanket over the top of it. Place a washable rug on the floor inside. Place either sweet (ice-cream or jam) or sour (lemons and limes) food items in some plastic bowls and provide spoons for tasting. Check for any allergies to the food items and substitute them accordingly.

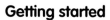

Getting started

- Take the children into the outdoor area, let them play outside and discover the den you have made! Ask them what they have found and be as surprised and excited as they are. Let the children play in the den, playing alongside them and asking questions about their play.
- Bring the bowls into the den and say *Look what I have found outside!* Allow the children to explore the items in the bowl and encourage them to use it in their imaginative play.
- Encourage them to smell what is in each bowl and identify whether the contents smell *sweet* or *sour.*

Development matters
Begin to make-believe by pretending.

Let's talk!

Use talk to describe what the children are doing by providing a running commentary, *Oh, I can see what you are doing, you are smelling the sweet jam.* For children requiring support, say *The lemon smells sour doesn't it?* and lift up the bowl with the lemon to the child's nose. For children requiring a challenge, ask *Can you find something that smells sweet?* Note how the children use make-believe play in the den, for example, they may use the bowls to do some pretend cooking!

Top tip

You as the key child's person are there to support them in exploring new situations and encouraging them to take risks.

Differentiation

This activity is suitable for children of all levels of ability because the children can enjoy playing in the den, using the food as a resource as required. Provide support by suggesting play themes to the children, *It's a really hot day and you like the ice-cream to cool you down!* Challenge children by asking them to tell you about other sweet or sour foodstuffs they would like to use in their play.

Further ideas

- Make another den indoors and include various items for imaginative play such as torches, maps, books, hats and mark-making materials.

Help babies develop an ability to listen for and respond to quiet sounds with this activity.

Setting up

Collect a variety of objects that are soft to touch, for example, a feather, a teddy bear, a piece of voile and a fluffy ball. Set up a cosy area with a rug, throw and cushions, either indoors or outdoors and place the objects in an attractive basket or box. Find a CD or tape of lullaby music.

Development matters

Respond to a range of familiar sounds, for example, turning to a sound source such as a voice.

Getting started

- Cuddle the baby either on your lap or sitting close together. Gently say the baby's name and sing or hum a song to the baby. Now play the CD or tape, playing the music very quietly.
- Take an object such as a feather and touch the baby's hand and face with it.
- Touch your hand and face as well with the feather, saying *This is soft – ahh, so soft. What a soft feather.*
- Follow on with the other objects, taking your time and watching the baby's responses. Touch your face gently and then the baby's face and say *Hush, hush, we are being very quiet today.*
- Finish the activity with a cuddle and a gentle song.

Let's talk

Be creative with the objects and have fun with the baby. For example, stroke the teddy with the feather and say *Let's stroke teddy's tummy, ahh, fluffy!* Remember to laugh and smile, maybe making up a little action song to complement what you are doing. For a baby needing support, keep your words simple *Teddy soft, soft teddy.* To challenge a baby, say *Where's the feather?* or *Where's the soft ball?* and point your finger at the object to help the baby look for it. Watch for the baby's reactions to each object, noticing the baby's body language and sounds that they make. Notice the voices and sounds that young babies respond to.

Top tip

This activity will provide the baby with the opportunity to form warm, caring attachments with you, their key person.

Differentiation

Keep the activity simple by encouraging the baby to look at you and listen to your voice. Babies requiring a challenge can choose objects from the basket themselves, encourage them to join you in saying *Shh* or *Hush.*

Further ideas

- Find toys that will make different sounds, such as a bell or a toy that squeaks, and talk to the babies about the sounds they make.
- Provide simple percussion instruments for the babies to explore.

Noisy box

Have fun exploring some noisy toys with the babies.

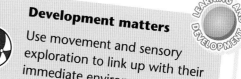

Development matters
Use movement and sensory exploration to link up with their immediate environment.

Setting up

Set up a cosy, quiet area with rugs, throws and cushions. Find a box with a lid, such as a large shoebox, decorate it with shiny paper, feathers, sequins and so on. Now place spoons of different sizes, a small saucepan with its lid and a small drum into the box. Place the box in the quiet area.

Getting started

- Sit on the rug, with the younger baby in your arms or place the baby on the cushions, ensuring their back is supported. Draw the baby's attention to the shoebox and either pick up the baby's hand and touch the box together or encourage the baby to touch the box independently.

- Either lift the lid with the baby's hand in yours or ask the baby to lift the lid. Look into the box together to see what's inside. Let the baby have some time to look into the box, while you sit quietly and watch. Take out the drum, say its name and bang on it a few times. Pick up the baby's hand and bang on the drum together or ask a more mobile baby to bang on the drum themselves.
- Investigate the items from the box one by one, talking to the baby about what they are and the sounds they make. Take your time, allowing the baby to look, touch and listen to the objects as you bang the spoons together or hit the saucepan and so on.
- If the baby is more mobile, sit back and let them explore and discover what is in the box by reaching in and picking up things. If the baby is made anxious by the noise, stop the activity and cuddle and reassure them.

Let's talk!

To provide support in the early stages, pick up the baby's hand, hold the spoon in your hand and the baby's and beat the saucepan, saying *We are making a noise with the spoon!* Later as a challenge, ask *Can you find the spoon and bang the saucepan with it?* Note what physical skills the baby uses to make contact with the objects, reaching, crawling and so on.

Top tip

As the baby's key person, you will be supporting the baby, helping to build their confidence in reaching into the box and taking things out.

Differentiation

This activity will improve the baby's coordination and manipulative skills. Provide support by letting the baby simply listen to the sounds each object makes in turn. Challenge other babies by asking them if they can place the lid back on the box and take it off again and then invite them to find a named item for you.

Further ideas

- Hang spoons, saucepans and musical instruments from a low curtain pole for babies to investigate and make noise with.

Let's make a noise

Make some noise together as you learn about relative size.

Setting up
Find a low table, appropriate for the age group and cover it with silver foil. Place the table either indoors or outdoors, in an area where there is plenty of space for the children to enjoy the activity. Now find some big and small saucepans and some big and small spoons and arrange them in an attractive way on the table. Place some cushions around the table for the children to sit on.

Development matters

Recognise big things and small things in meaningful contexts.

Getting started
- Encourage the children to join you in the activity by picking up a spoon and beating it on a saucepan saying, *Come and listen to the noise I can make with the spoon.* Let the children explore and investigate the resources, now and again commenting on what they are doing, *I am enjoying listening to the noise you are making.*
- Now talk about big and small saying *Can you find me a big saucepan?* or *Where is the small spoon?* Invite the children to make different noises with the resources, introducing a pattern such as two loud noises followed by two quiet ones.
- Let the children bang, tap and make a noise with the resources, you can join in too!

Let's talk
Talk to the children about what they are doing to help them begin to link words with actions. For example, *You are banging on the big saucepan with the little spoon.* For children needing support, hold on to their hand and pick up a spoon together, saying *We are tapping the big saucepan* or *We are holding the small spoon.* For children requiring a challenge, ask *Can you find a little saucepan and hit it with a big spoon?*

Top tip
The children will greatly benefit from you playing alongside them during the activity. Not only will you be supporting their language development, but you will also be building positive relationships with them.

Differentiation
Provide support by letting the children choose what they want to make a noise with. To challenge children, ask them to find other big things and small things to make a noise with.

Further ideas
- Fill a saucepan with 'gloop' made from cornflour and water and let the children spoon the mixture in and out of the saucepan.
- Provide other kitchen equipment that can make a noise in the home corner for the children to enjoy as they play there.

Clap, clap your hands

Introduce this copying and imitating game for young children to enjoy.

Setting up
Set up a cosy area with rugs and cushions either indoors or outdoors.

Getting started

Development matters

Build relationships with special people.

Respond to words and interactive rhymes, such as 'Clap Hands'.

- Sit down with the children in the cosy area and say *We are going to play a clapping game today* and start clapping with your hands. Encourage the children to join in with you.
- Pause from clapping so that you can hear the children clap and say *Well done, you are clapping your hands and making a noise.* Now say *Clap your hands and touch your nose, clap your hands and touch your toes* and make the actions as you say this.
- Make this a fun action game with the children, making your voice loud, soft and saying the rhyme fast and then slowly. As the children become more confident, encourage them to move around as you play the game, saying *Can you walk and clap your hands?* or *Jump and clap your hands!*

Let's talk
Encourage the children to say *Clap, clap* as they say the rhyme and copy your actions. For support, say the child's name and *Well done, you are clapping your hands together.* For children needing a challenge, say *Can you count how many times we clap, one, two, three?* Note how the children respond to the game and how they join in with the actions.

Top tip
You can keep the children's interest in the game for longer by making it fun, pretend to make a mistake, for example, and touch your hair instead of your toes. Young children will enjoy this and you will maintain their attention.

Differentiation
To provide support hold a child's hands and clap together. Make it more challenging by asking the children to incorporate movement into the clapping following your direction as you introduce new ideas.

Further ideas
- Use instruments such as bells or drums and play a copying game with the children, rattle your bell once and ask them to copy you, then shake it twice and so on.
- Invite children to clap along to familiar rhymes such as 'Clap hands, clap hands' and 'Pat-a-cake'.

Tipping towers

Have fun building tall towers, knocking them down and listening to the sounds it makes!

Setting up
Collect together resources that the children could build towers with, for example, different-sized cardboard boxes, building blocks and Duplo. Fill a basket with small bells. Set up an area for the activity either indoors or outdoors.

Development matters
Are interested in pushing and pulling things, and begin to build structures.

Getting started
- Sit down in the area and begin to build a tower yourself with the boxes, encouraging some children to come and join you. Let the children choose what they want to build their towers with. They might want to start with a box and then place some large building blocks and finally a piece of Duplo.
- Say *I'm going to knock my tower down – crash!* Knock your tower down as you say this and keep emphasising the noise it makes *crash, bang* or *clap*.
- Encourage the children to build towers of their choice and then knock them down, keeping your commentary running about the noise the towers make as they fall down. Now ask the children to choose a bell from the basket. Ask the children to shake their bell and listen to the sound it makes.
- Say *Can you place your bell on top of your tower?* and model this action on the tower that you have built. Ask, *What can you hear now when you knock you tower down?* Let the children experiment with building tall or small towers and placing different bells on top.

Let's talk
For children needing support, say *Your tower makes a loud noise when it falls down* or *Your bell rings loudly when it falls down.* To challenge children, say *Tell me about the noise your tower makes when it falls down* or *What does your bell do when it falls down?* Notice what the children enjoy building with and how high they can successfully build their towers, taking care to balance the boxes and bricks.

Top tip
Encourage the children to build their towers as high as they can as this will support their physical development and coordination.

Differentiation
To keep the activity simple, choose one resource for the children to build with, for example, building blocks of the same size. Challenge children by inviting them to add specific blocks or bricks to their towers such as, two large blue blocks and then two small red bricks.

Further ideas
- Provide craft materials and invite the children to decorate the cardboard boxes before they build their towers.
- Give the children other construction toys and invite them to build different-sized buildings to add to road or play mats.

Squelch, squelch

Let the children find out what sounds some familiar materials make with this activity.

Setting up

Collect five builder's trays and place a different material in each one, for example, wet paper, cooked spaghetti, wet compost, rice and tissue paper and so on. Create an area outdoors where you can place the trays and allow the children plenty of space to become involved in the activity. Check for allergies to any of the resources.

Getting started

- Ensure that the children are wearing outdoor clothing and their wellies. Take them outside and show them the trays, saying *Look what I have found outside today!*
- Talk to the children about what is in each tray, giving lots of praise when they tell you what the materials are. Invite the children to jump into the trays and jump in with them! Talk about the sounds you can hear and encourage the children to tell you the sounds.
- Encourage the children to jump into each tray in turn and compare the different sounds they can make. Supervise the children closely, so that they don't slip as they jump into the trays.

Let's talk

Keep your commentary running, asking the children what they can hear. For those children requiring support, hold their hand and help them jump into the tray, saying *Can you hear the squidgy sound the compost makes?* To challenge children, say *Tell me what you can hear when you jump into the tray.* Note the comments that the children are making as they jump into each tray.

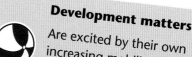

Development matters

Are excited by their own increasing mobility and often set their own challenges.

Explore by repeating patterns of play.

Top tip

Remember that children learn by doing and exploring their environment. As they watch you and other children, jump in and out of the trays, this will help build their confidence and strong relationships.

Differentiation

Provide support by having just one or two trays for the children to jump in and out of. Challenge children by asking, *Can you jump into the tray with the compost and then into the tray with paper in it?*

Further ideas

- Take the trays indoors and let the children sit at a table and explore the materials further with their hands.
- Provide a range of modelling materials for the children to investigate such as play dough, clay and cornflour and water 'gloop'.

Floating bubbles

Play this game to show children that sounds can be quiet and soft as well as loud.

Setting up
Provide some pots of bubble mix. Check that children are not allergic to the mixture.

Development matters

Have favourite stories, rhymes, songs, poems or jingles.

Getting started
- Take the children into the outdoor area, ensuring that they are wearing suitable clothing. Ask the children to choose a favourite song or nursery rhyme to sing and sing a couple of the songs chosen by the children. Encourage the children to enjoy marching, jumping or skipping as you sing, joining in with them too.
- Take a pot of bubbles and blow them into the air. Ask the children to sing another song as they watch the bubbles go up in the air. Ask *Do bubbles make a noise?* Listen to their comments, play a game that when a bubble pops they clap their hands or whisper their name.
- Choose another favourite song to end the activity.

Let's talk
Keep your commentary running as you talk about the bubbles, how they go up in the air, pop, their colours and so on. For children needing support, point to the bubbles and say *Can you catch the bubbles in the air?* To challenge children, ask *Can you tell me what the bubbles are doing?* Notice what the child chooses to sing and share this with the parents, asking them to sing the songs or rhymes at home.

Top tip
This activity helps children to become aware that they can choose songs they like and sing them. As the supportive adult, you are giving them praise and encouragement to do so.

Differentiation
Support children by singing a song together that is familiar to them and let them enjoy catching the bubbles in the air. To challenge children, give them their own pot of bubbles to blow and ask them to sing a song and blow the bubbles.

Further ideas
- Put the bubble mixture into a bowl and let the children blow through straws to make big bubbles.
- Mix the bubbles with a little paint and let the children make pictures, blowing down a straw into the bubbles to create a colourful bubble picture.

Musical basket walk

Take the children on a walk-about to look for musical instruments.

Setting up
Fill some baskets with a selection of musical instruments. Place the baskets around the setting, both indoors and outdoors.

Getting started
- Say *Let's go on a walk today and play some music on our way.* Now start walking around your setting and encourage some children to follow you. Walk to a basket of instruments, take one out and start playing it. Encourage the children to take an instrument out of the basket and play it.
- As the children play the instruments, comment about the sounds they make: *Listen to the big bang of your drum* or *Those bells are tinkling*. Now carry on walking around your setting and let the children find the baskets of instruments, each time stopping to play them.

Let's talk!
Remember to allow time for the children to play the instruments and talk to you about the sounds they hear. For children requiring support, help them to choose an instrument and tell them the name of it, *Listen to the sound the triangle makes, ting, ting.* To challenge children, ask them to tell you the name of the instrument and what sound it makes, *Tell me about what you can hear.* Note the words the children use to call the instruments and what words they use to describe them.

Top tip
This activity will help children become familiar with the layout of the setting and will reinforce their sense of belonging to it.

Differentiation
Support children by finding just one basket and enjoying the instruments there. To challenge children, let them take the instruments out of the basket and play them as they walk to find the next basket, leave those instruments there and pick up some new ones to walk on with.

Further ideas
- Show the children how to make shakers from empty boxes by filling them with peas or lentils and decorating them. Seal the lids with Sellotape or glue.
- Provide a range of percussion instruments for the children to join in when you share a favourite song.

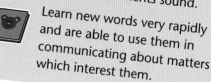

Development matters

Show an interest in the way musical instruments sound.

Learn new words very rapidly and are able to use them in communicating about matters which interest them.

This activity offers a chance for babies to explore and taste porridge.

Setting up

Make some porridge with water, ensuring that it is of a soft consistency, not too runny. You will need to make enough to fill the bottom of an empty water tray (only about 1cm deep). Check that there are no babies with an allergy to oats. If so, you could use cornflour and water to make a similar mix. This activity is suitable for babies from three months onwards.

Development matters

Explore the space around them through movements of hands and feet and by rolling.

Communicate in a variety of ways including crying, gurgling, babbling and squealing.

Getting started

- First, ensure that the room is warm as you need to strip the baby down to their nappy for this activity. Carefully, sit the baby in the water tray filled with porridge. You will need to hold younger babies or supervise older babies very carefully.
- Let the baby explore the space around them as well as the porridge with both their hands and feet. The baby may want to taste the porridge, if so, talk to them about it, saying *You are tasting the porridge!*
- If the baby is not mobile, you can play with the porridge and let the baby watch you. Remember to keep talking to the baby as you let the mixture run through your fingers and show them the porridge at their eye level for them to focus on.

Let's talk!

Keep your commentary running as the baby plays with the porridge making eye contact as you speak. For babies requiring support, hold the baby's hand and touch the porridge, saying *Look what we can do with our hands!* To challenge a baby, make marks in the porridge and watch and see if the baby copies you. Notice the movements the baby makes and how they use their hands and feet to explore the porridge.

Top tip

This activity will allow a baby to explore materials at their own rate of development. You are there to support and ensure the baby feels safe as they explore the world around them.

Differentiation

Provide support by holding on to the baby as they play with the porridge. To challenge a baby, you can put a ball in the porridge and encourage the baby to reach for it.

Further ideas

- Provide other textured food for babies to explore with their fingers.

Snuggle up for some fun finding out about a range of vegetables together.

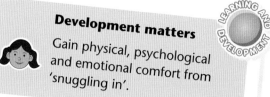

Development matters

Gain physical, psychological and emotional comfort from 'snuggling in'.

Setting up

Cut up pieces of a range of vegetables of different shapes and colours and put them in a basket. Check for allergies to the vegetables. Set up a cosy area with rugs and cushions and place the basket here. You can also have a CD or tape to end the activity with some gentle lullaby music. This activity is suitable for babies from six months onwards.

Getting started

- Start by simply cuddling the baby and being still and quiet. Say the baby's name and sing a song quietly. Now pick out a piece of vegetable from the basket and hold it up for the baby to see and touch. Say *We are touching some cauliflower*. Hold the cauliflower to the baby's mouth so that they can touch it with their tongue or taste it. Supervise the baby at all times and make sure they are able to chew and swallow the vegetables safely.
- Carry on doing this with the other vegetables, enjoying a snuggling time with the baby. For the more mobile baby, cuddle them as they choose the vegetables from the basket themselves and play with them.
- Finish with a song or play some lullaby music.

Let's talk!

During this activity, you should have quiet moments where you and the baby are enjoying each other's company. For a baby who needs support, take the pieces of vegetable out of the basket one at a time and show them to the baby in turn. If a baby requires a challenge, say *Can you find me the tomato? Where's some cabbage?* Note how the baby responds to attention, such as making eye contact or making noises.

Top tip

If the baby plays and reaches for the vegetables from the basket by themselves, let them know you are there to support them by talking to them. They will know that their key person is near by and feel safe and loved.

Differentiation

To provide support, spend more time cuddling the baby and maybe just looking at one type of vegetable and tasting it or licking it. To challenge children, keep moving the basket away, so the baby has to reach further to take a vegetable out of it.

Further ideas

- Provide a sofa or comfy chair so that you, the baby and their parents can sit together.
- Create a cosy area in your book corner with large beanbags and cushions so that babies and their key people can snuggle in at story time.

Tongue fantastic

Explore what sounds your mouths can make together.

Setting up

Make a cosy area with rugs and cushions, either indoors or outdoors. Ensure that you set the area up in a quiet space, so that the activity can be enjoyed without disruption.

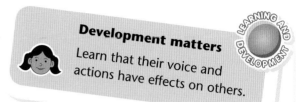

Development matters

Learn that their voice and actions have effects on others.

Getting started

- Gather the children together to play a game. Ensure younger babies are supported by a cushion or hold them in your lap. Now say *I wonder who can copy what I do?* and show the children your tongue. Encourage the children to copy you, giving praise when they do, and saying *I can see your tongue!*

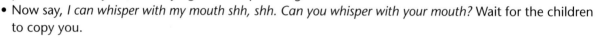

- Now say, *I can whisper with my mouth shh, shh. Can you whisper with your mouth?* Wait for the children to copy you.
- Next say *I can laugh with my mouth haa, haa* and laugh. Again, wait for the children to copy you, repeating the activity if necessary until they join in.
- Carry on the game by doing other actions with your mouth, such as singing, making a loud noise and so on for as long as the children's attention is held.

Let's talk!

This activity aids speech development as the babies are finding out what their mouths can do. To provide support repeat the actions and say what you are doing until the child joins in, *This is my tongue. Where's your tongue? Can you show me your tongue? Where is it?* To challenge a child ask them to do two actions with their mouth, such as *Can you whisper and then shout?* and demonstrate these actions to them. Notice how the child observes your actions and those of the other children.

Top tip

Each child's speech development proceeds at its own rate. This activity will help children to become more aware of themselves and what they can do.

Differentiation

For children needing support, just make a couple of actions with your mouth, such as smiling or whispering. Challenge children by asking them to show you what they can do with their mouths and then copying their actions.

Further ideas

- Play the copying game to music, changing the tempo from fast to slow to make a fun game!
- Start to share familiar nursery rhymes together, encouraging the children to copy you, joining in with repetitive phrases and words.

Hooray for purées

Introduce some new flavours to children with this tasty activity.

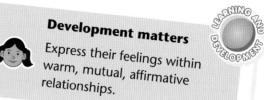

Development matters

Express their feelings within warm, mutual, affirmative relationships.

Setting up

Collect a range of fruit and vegetables, such as strawberries, kiwis, bananas and carrots and make them into purées. Check for any allergies. Place each purée into a separate bowl and put the bowls on a low lying table. You will also need some disposable plastic spoons.

Getting started

- Gather the children around the table, you may need to hold younger children in your lap. Tell the children that you are going to try some different purées today. Take a spoon and taste one of the purées yourself, saying *Mmm, strawberry purée!* Then either take a clean spoon and hold it to the child's mouth or give the child the spoon to try the purée themselves.
- Continue to do this with the other flavours, remembering not to rush the activity and allowing the babies to take their time to try each one in turn. Talk about the different flavours and colours you can see and compare the flavours.
- To finish the activity, let the children play with and explore the purées by themselves, either with spoons or their fingers.

Let's talk!

Try and keep a balance of sometimes commenting on what the child is doing and then sitting quietly to listen for their comments on the purée. For children needing support say, *Well done, strawberry, mmm* as you hold the spoon to their mouth. For children requiring a challenge, say *I wonder which purée you are trying now? What does it taste like?* Notice the child's likes and dislikes and share this information with their parents.

Top tip

As the child's key person, you have a close relationship with them and you can encourage them to tell you if they like or dislike the purée.

Differentiation

Provide support by limiting the activity to two distinct flavours and colours, perhaps kiwi and strawberry. To challenge children, let them choose the purée they want to try for themselves, saying *Who can find the apple purée?*

Further ideas

- Place the purée in trays and let the babies mark make and make patterns in it.
- Introduce different purées at snack time for the children to try.

Let the children use a variety of fruit to get colourfully creative.

Setting up

Set up a low table ready for use. Put a different colour paint of your choice in each of three trays and place the trays on the table. Provide sheets of paper. Cut up a variety of fruit, such as bananas, kiwis and apples and place in a plastic bowl on the table. Keep a small selection of the fruit aside to taste afterwards. Check if any children have allergies to the fruit.

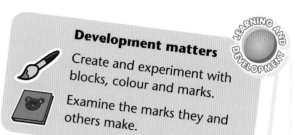

Development matters

Create and experiment with blocks, colour and marks.

Examine the marks they and others make.

Getting started

- Gather the children at the table and show them the colourful paint you have chosen. Hold up pieces of the different fruit in turn, saying what it is or asking the children if they can identify it. Ask, *Who would like to paint with fruit today?*
- Now take a piece of fruit, dip it in the paint and make a print or pattern on some paper. Invite the children to take a piece of fruit, choose a paint colour and make their own patterns on paper. Supervise at all times to make sure the children don't put the painted fruit in their mouths.
- Let the children continue to investigate making patterns as long as they are interested in doing so. Comment on the patterns they make and the colours they choose.
- When the activity has been cleared away offer the children pieces of the fruit to taste. Encourage the children to name the fruit, giving them lots of praise when they do. As they enjoy tasting the fruit encourage them to recall what patterns they made and which fruit was easier/harder than others to use to print with.

Let's talk!

Keep using the name of the fruit as the children are painting with it. For support, talk to the children about their patterns, *Look at the marks your kiwi has made!* For children requiring a challenge, ask *Can you tell me about the patterns you are making with your fruit?* Notice how the children's fine manipulative skills are developed as they pick up the fruit and print with it.

Top tip

This activity allows each child to make marks and be creative at their own rate of development. Use fruits from the children's own cultures or countries.

Differentiation

Support children by using one type of fruit, for example, an apple and demonstrate a pattern for the child to copy. To challenge children ask them if they can make different patterns with the fruit, for example, *Can you make a swirling pattern with some banana?*

Further ideas

- Provide a selection of different fruits and vegetables and let the children sort them for colour or size.
- Try printing with foam pieces cut into specific shapes and make repeating patterns.

A taste of goodness

Let the children help you to make a fruit salad to share with this activity.

Setting up

Gather a range of different fruit, pineapples, mangoes, bananas and so on. Find a really large bowl and place it on a low table. You will need a sharp knife to cut up the fruit (for adult use and with close supervision at all times). Have small bowls and spoons ready to eat the fruit salad afterwards. Check that children are not allergic to the fruits.

Development matters
Develop confidence in own abilities.

Getting started

- Gather the children around the table and say that you are going to make a fruit salad together today. Ask, *Who likes to eat fruit?* Wait for the children's responses, giving praise and encouragement when they talk about fruits they like to eat.
- Now hold up a fruit such as the kiwi, say its name and start to peel it and cut it up remembering to tell the children that while you are using a sharp knife they need to sit very still. Pass some pieces of kiwi around the group for the children to try. Ask them to tell you if they like it or not. Now cut up some more kiwi fruit and ask the children to place the fruit in the large bowl.
- Continue to do this with the other fruits until you have placed all the cut-up fruit in the large bowl, add some apple juice or water to finish the fruit salad. Remind the children what you have done, peeling and chopping the fruit to make a fruit salad.
- Serve the fruit salad in small bowls with spoons at snack time or mealtime.

Let's talk

For children requiring support, hold on to their hand as they place the fruit in the bowl. Saying, *Well done, you are making a fruit salad.* For children requiring a challenge ask them *Can you help me count how many different fruits we have in the fruit salad?* and count along with them. Note which fruit the children like and dislike and share this information with parents.

Top tip

Keep this session short and enjoyable so that a child doesn't lose interest in the activity. If a child does not want to eat any of the fruit, just reassure them that they don't have to and let them watch the activity.

Differentiation

Provide support by just having a few familiar types of fruit for the children to taste and place in the fruit salad. For children requiring a challenge let them break off sections of fruit such as an orange that you have peeled to add to the fruit salad themselves.

Further ideas

- Make the fruit salad towards the end of the day and let parents try it when they collect their children. The children will enjoy and gain confidence from hearing their parents' feedback.

Five a day

Encourage the children to enjoy healthy eating with this tasty idea.

Setting up

You will need a large tin of sweetcorn, a chopped-up cucumber, a few cherry tomatoes and a sliced red pepper. Place the ingredients on a large tray. You will also need a large plastic bowl and some large spoons. Place all of the items on a low table. Check for children who may be allergic to any of the ingredients.

Development matters
Are beginning to understand variations in size.

Getting started

- Talk about eating healthy foods with the children and ask if they know we should have five pieces of fruit or vegetable every day to keep healthy. Ask if they know the names of any fruits and vegetables.
- Tell the children that you are going to make a sweetcorn salad today. Show them all the ingredients one by one and tell them what each is called. Now say *Who would like to taste the sweetcorn?* and pass the tray around for the children to taste the sweetcorn.
- Repeat this with all the ingredients, keeping your commentary running *We are tasting the tomatoes* and so on.
- Now talk to the children about the size of the various ingredients. Saying, *Which is bigger, the sweetcorn or the pepper?* or The *sweetcorn is smaller than the cucumber.*
- Give each child a spoon and encourage them to pick up the ingredients from the tray and put them into the bowl together to make a salad to share together at snack or mealtimes.

Let's talk

For children needing support say *You are holding a tiny piece of sweetcorn* and give them praise as they tip the sweetcorn into the bowl. For children requiring a challenge ask them, *Which is the biggest pieces of vegetable we have here? Can you show me the smallest?* Note the observations that the children are making about the sizes of the ingredients.

Top tip

Remember that a warm, trusting relationship with knowledgeable adults supports children's learning more effectively than any amount of resources.

Differentiation

Keep this activity simple by talking about the size of one or two vegetables only and holding on to the child's hand as they tip the vegetables into the bowl. To challenge children, ask them to find you something that is tiny like the sweetcorn or something that is bigger like the tomato.

Further ideas

- Ask the children to draw pictures of the different salad items, noticing the colours of the actual food.
- Share a picture book about fruit and vegetables with the children and compare the pictures with the salad items you have used.